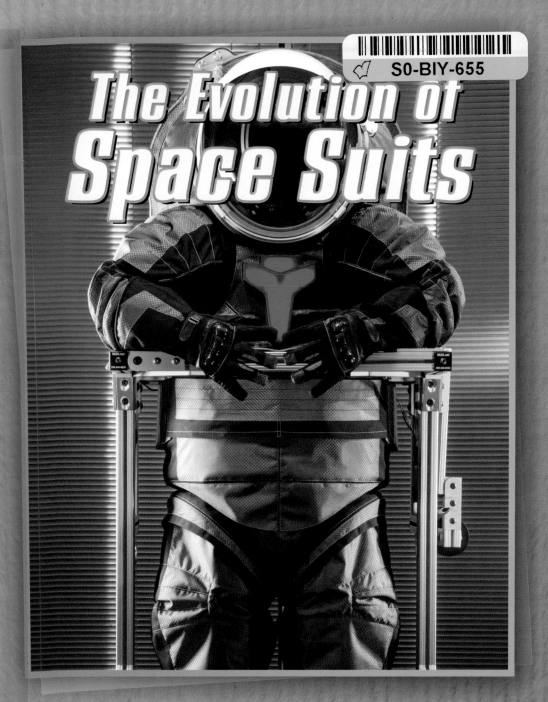

The Evolution of Space Suits

Danica Kassebaum

EMMA S. CLARK MEMORIAL LIBRARY
Setauket, New York 11733

✷ Smithsonian

© 2019 Smithsonian Institution. The name "Smithsonian" and the Smithsonian logo are registered trademarks owned by the Smithsonian Institution.

S0-BIY-655

Contributing Author

Heather Schultz, M.A.

Consultants

Cathleen Lewis
Museum Curator, Space History
Chair, Division of Space History
National Air and Space Museum

Tamieka Grizzle, Ed.D.
K–5 STEM Lab Instructor
Harmony Leland Elementary School

Stephanie Anastasopoulos, M.Ed.
TOSA, STREAM Integration
Solana Beach School District

Publishing Credits

Rachelle Cracchiolo, M.S.Ed., *Publisher*

Conni Medina, M.A.Ed., *Managing Editor*

Diana Kenney, M.A.Ed., NBCT, *Series Developer*

Véronique Bos, *Creative Director*

June Kikuchi, *Content Director*

Robin Erickson, *Art Director*

Seth Rogers, *Editor*

Mindy Duits, *Senior Graphic Designer*

Smithsonian Science Education Center

Image Credits: front cover, p.1, p.7 (bottom), p.18 (bottom) © Smithsonian; p.5 De Rocker/Alamy; p.6 Everett Historical/Shutterstock; p.7 (top) SZ Photo/Scherl/Bridgeman Images; p.8, p.9, p.10 (left), p.11 (all), p.12 (all), p.13, p.14, p.15, p.17 (middle), p.18 (middle left and right), p.19 (all), p. 20 (all), p. 21 (all), p.22, p.23 (all), p. 24 (right), p.25, p.27 (bottom), p.31 NASA; p.10 (right) RIA Novosti/Science Source; p.16 (left) Joseph Sohm / Shutterstock; p.16 (bottom) NASA/ Science Source; p.17 (bottom) Steve Jurvetson; p.24 (left) Jim Olive/Polaris/Newscom; all other images from iStock and/or Shutterstock.

Library of Congress Cataloging-in-Publication Data

Names: Kassebaum, Danica, author.
Title: The evolution of space suits / Danica Kassebaum.
Description: Huntington Beach, CA : Teacher Created Materials, [2018] | Audience: Grades 4 to 6. | Includes index. |
Identifiers: LCCN 2018006368 (print) | LCCN 2018008975 (ebook) | ISBN 9781493869404 (E-book) | ISBN 9781493867004 (pbk.)
Subjects: LCSH: Space suits--Design and construction--Juvenile literature. |
Life support systems (Space environment)--Juvenile literature. | Aerospace
engineering--Juvenile literature. | Manned space
flight--History--Juvenile
literature. 7446171
Classification: LCC TL1550 (ebook) | LCC TL1550 .K37 2018 (print) | DDC 629.47/72--dc23
LC record available at https://lccn.loc.gov/2018006368

Smithsonian

© 2019 Smithsonian Institution. The name "Smithsonian" and the Smithsonian logo are registered trademarks owned by the Smithsonian Institution.

Teacher Created Materials

5301 Oceanus Drive
Huntington Beach, CA 92649-1030
www.tcmpub.com
ISBN 978-1-4938-6700-4
©2019 Teacher Created Materials, Inc.
Printed in China
Nordica.072018.CA21800844

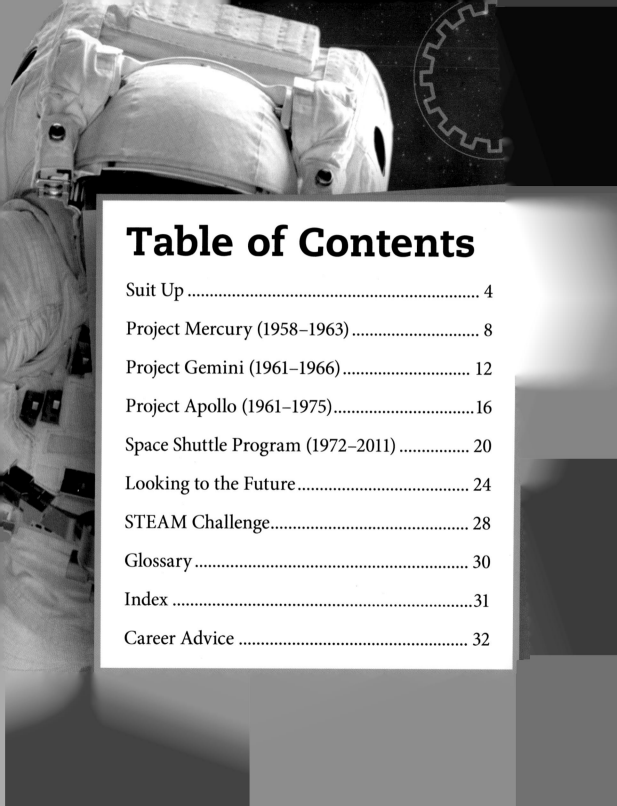

Table of Contents

Suit Up 4

Project Mercury (1958–1963) 8

Project Gemini (1961–1966) 12

Project Apollo (1961–1975) 16

Space Shuttle Program (1972–2011) 20

Looking to the Future 24

STEAM Challenge 28

Glossary 30

Index 31

Career Advice 32

Suit Up

Imagine stepping outside on the coldest day of the year. What would you wear? Most likely, you would wear something to protect yourself from the freezing wind and cold. Now, imagine stepping outside on the hottest day of the year. Would you wear the same thing? Of course you wouldn't. On Earth, people change the way they dress depending on the weather.

Now, what if you were in space? The conditions in space are much more extreme than they are on Earth. Humans would not last long in space without special clothes. So, engineers developed suits just for astronauts.

Many different space suits have been made over the years. They were designed to help astronauts do their jobs in space. These suits have different features that help astronauts do different things. But the main job of every space suit is the same—keep the person inside safe.

The coldest temperature ever recorded on Earth was –89 degrees Celsius (–128 degrees Fahrenheit). The temperature in deep space is –271°C (–455°F).

This suit was worn by the first human in space.

Building a Suit

In the early days of space research, people knew very little about what it was like among the stars. Most of what they learned, they learned from experience. Early pilots knew that air became colder as they flew higher. Flight suits were made to keep pilots warm. At first, they just wore heavy jackets. As airplanes flew higher, pilots found it harder to breathe. This is because the air is thinner at higher **altitudes**. There is less oxygen to breathe.

Later, flight suits became special full-body suits with masks. The masks gave pilots oxygen to breathe, while the suits put pressure on their bodies similar to the pressure felt on the ground. The first space suits were modeled after these pressure suits.

Today's space suits are the result of years of research. But they were not always this advanced. It took a lot of hard work by scientists and engineers to create the space suits used today.

Pilot Amelia Earhart wears a flight suit.

Earhart wears a heavy jacket and head gear.

Early pilots used to fly hot-air balloons to run experiments at high altitudes. At the time, balloons could fly much higher than airplanes could.

an early pressure suit used in an airplane

Project Mercury (1958-1963)

The first U.S. space program was called Project Mercury. Its goal was to send a person into space, orbit Earth, and return home safely. At the time, scientists in the Soviet Union had their own plans to send a man into space. Each country wanted to succeed before the other did. This competition was known as the Space Race.

Project Mercury began in the U.S. Air Force. But it was soon moved to the National Aeronautics and Space Administration (NASA). The focus of the program was to study space and compete with the Soviet Union. The Soviets had already sent a satellite into space. NASA needed to work quickly to keep up.

Scientists at NASA knew they needed to build a suit that would keep a person safe in space. They did not know for sure what a space suit would need. No one had ever been so far away from Earth. Scientists knew that a space suit would need to work like a pressure suit. But they would need to make some changes.

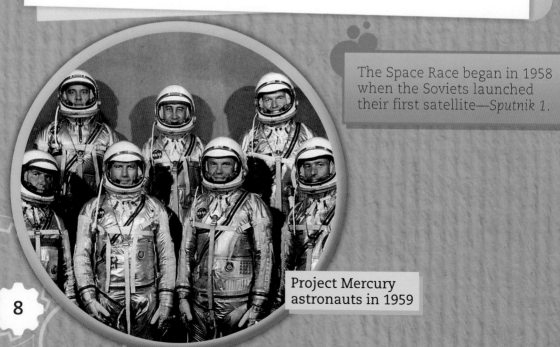

The Space Race began in 1958 when the Soviets launched their first satellite—*Sputnik 1*.

Project Mercury astronauts in 1959

NASA Langley Research Center in Virginia (above) was the main site of Project Mercury before operations moved to Texas.

The first space suit was made with **nylon** and neoprene—a type of rubber and the same material used for **wet suits**. It was coated with aluminum, which gave the space suit a shiny, silver look. This coating helped keep the suit warm on the inside. The silver suits became popular. Movies about space travel showed actors in silver space suits. This helped make space travel popular, too.

Mercury astronauts went into space, but they did not exit the spacecraft during their trips. Their space suits were only for traveling into space and back. Since the craft was pressurized, the space suits were kept unpressurized during flight. The suits only needed to pressurize if the ship failed. If astronauts were going to get out of the ships, they would need better suits.

Project Mercury was a success. But the Soviets were the first to send a man into orbit. His name was Yuri Gagarin (YOOR-ee guh-GAH-rin). About 10 months later, NASA sent John Glenn into orbit.

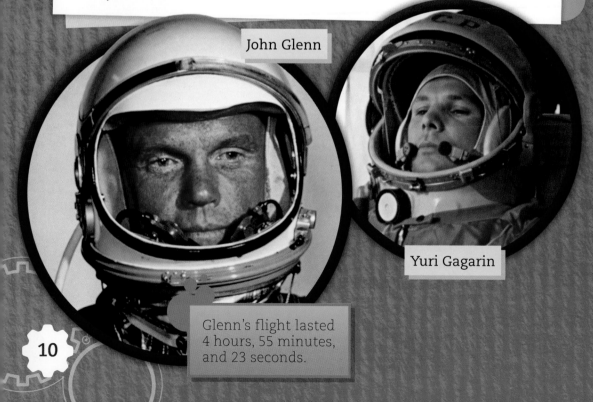

John Glenn

Yuri Gagarin

Glenn's flight lasted 4 hours, 55 minutes, and 23 seconds.

Mercury astronaut, and first American in space, Alan Shepard, gets helped into his space suit before flight.

Project Gemini (1961–1966)

In 1961, NASA began two more space projects. They were Projects Gemini and Apollo. Gemini was the next step in space travel. It had several goals.

First, scientists wanted to figure out how astronauts could stay in space for more than just a few hours. The goal was to keep astronauts in space for two weeks. Next, they wanted to see whether two spacecraft could come together while in space. The third goal would require a brand-new space suit. Scientists wanted to send an astronaut out of the spacecraft while in space.

Apollo 4 launches in 1967.

Ed White

A total of 12 flights were sent into space during Project Gemini. The first two flights were unmanned. During the fourth flight, Ed White became the first U.S. astronaut to walk in space. Again, the Soviets had beaten the United States. They had completed the **maneuver** three months earlier. But NASA followed with three more **spacewalks** before the Soviets could do a second. The Space Race continued.

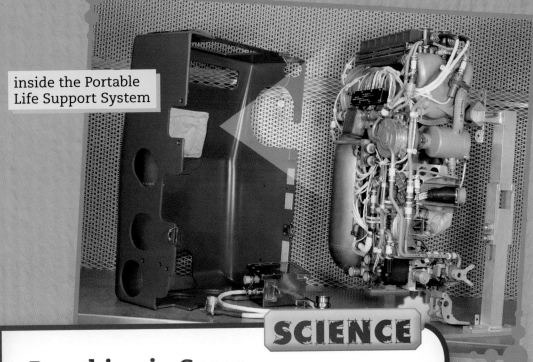

inside the Portable Life Support System

SCIENCE

Breathing in Space

When humans breathe, they inhale oxygen and exhale carbon dioxide. In space, there is no oxygen. So, scientists created a special backpack and filled it with oxygen. It used a fan to circulate oxygen through the space suit. It also removed carbon dioxide from the suit. This is how astronauts were able to breathe in space. It was called the Portable **Life Support** System.

The Gemini suit had to work in the spacecraft. But it also had to work outside the craft. Scientists at NASA changed the space suit. They attached a cord to the suit. The cord was connected to a life support system on the craft. It let them travel outside the ship while still being safe. These space suits were more advanced than the Mercury suits. They also had a better range of motion.

Ed White floats in space.

The Gemini space suits had six different layers of nylon. With these new suits, astronauts could stay outside the spacecraft for up to an hour. Astronaut Ed White's spacewalk lasted for 23 minutes.

On the final Gemini flight, astronaut Edwin "Buzz" Aldrin performed three spacewalks. He was in space for over five hours! This was a huge step forward in the Space Race.

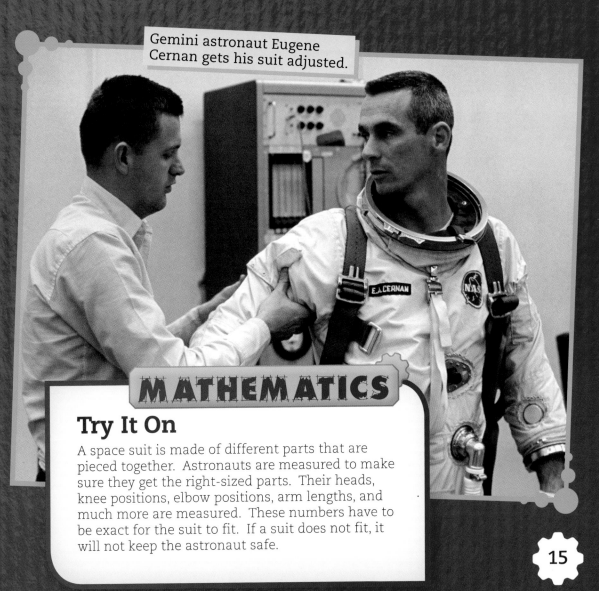

Gemini astronaut Eugene Cernan gets his suit adjusted.

MATHEMATICS

Try It On

A space suit is made of different parts that are pieced together. Astronauts are measured to make sure they get the right-sized parts. Their heads, knee positions, elbow positions, arm lengths, and much more are measured. These numbers have to be exact for the suit to fit. If a suit does not fit, it will not keep the astronaut safe.

Project Apollo (1961–1975)

Apollo 1 was meant to be the first manned flight of the Apollo spacecraft. But a tragic fire took the lives of the three men on board during the final test before takeoff.

Apollo 1 taught NASA a lesson. Scientists needed to make sure their astronauts were safe. Safety was more important than speed. It was almost two years before another crew went into space. In that time, NASA sent three unmanned ships into space. Then, in 1968, Apollo astronauts succeeded. They were in space for 11 days. This and other flights led to NASA's biggest test yet: sending men to the moon.

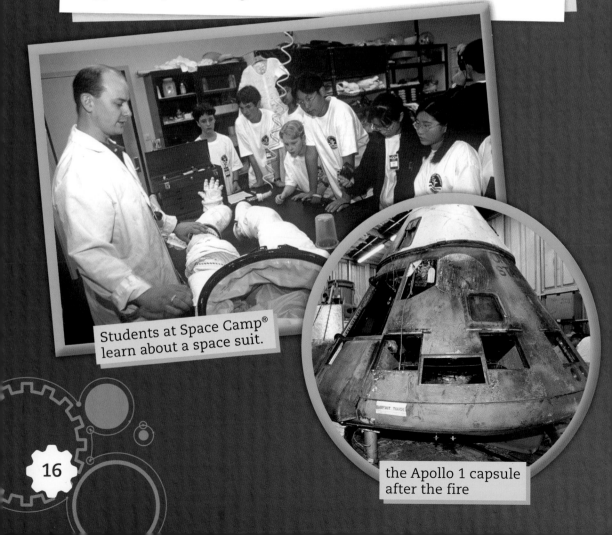

Students at Space Camp® learn about a space suit.

the Apollo 1 capsule after the fire

On July 20, 1969, Apollo 11 made history. It landed on the moon. Neil Armstrong and Buzz Aldrin stepped out and became the first people to walk on its surface. Americans had beaten the Soviets!

Project Apollo didn't end there. There were another six planned trips to the moon. All except one made it. Apollo 13 had to **abort** its mission early and only circled the moon.

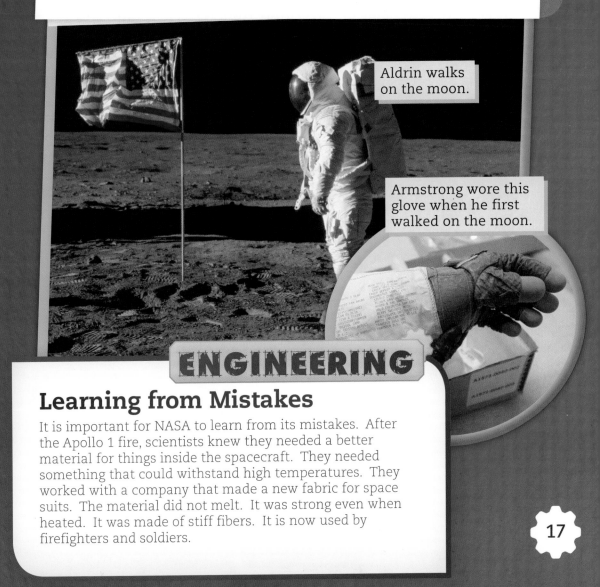

Aldrin walks on the moon.

Armstrong wore this glove when he first walked on the moon.

ENGINEERING

Learning from Mistakes

It is important for NASA to learn from its mistakes. After the Apollo 1 fire, scientists knew they needed a better material for things inside the spacecraft. They needed something that could withstand high temperatures. They worked with a company that made a new fabric for space suits. The material did not melt. It was strong even when heated. It was made of stiff fibers. It is now used by firefighters and soldiers.

The Apollo astronauts were the first people to walk on the moon. To do so, they had to be able to bend and move. They planned to pick up rocks while they were there. Engineers made special boots called overshoes for the moonwalk. These boots were made to protect feet from sharp rocks and extreme temperatures on the **lunar** surface. There was even an extra layer of material added for safety.

To be able to walk on the moon, astronauts needed special equipment. Engineers made a portable life-support system. This allowed astronauts to travel away from the spacecraft. These suits weighed 127 kilograms (280 pounds) on Earth and took up to 45 minutes to put on.

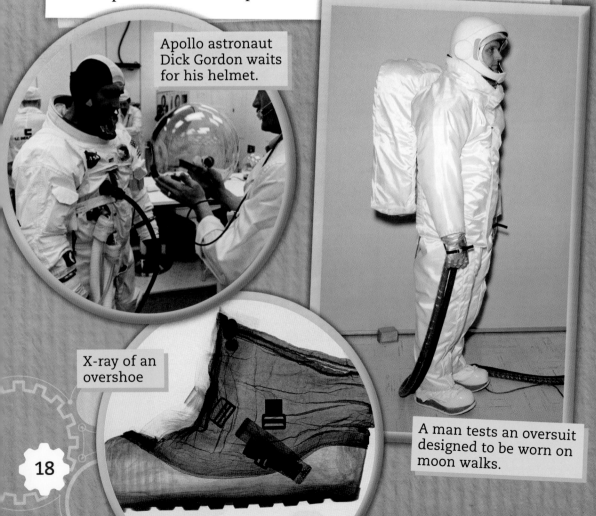

Apollo astronaut Dick Gordon waits for his helmet.

X-ray of an overshoe

A man tests an oversuit designed to be worn on moon walks.

Since the heavy suits were sealed, there was nowhere for astronauts' body heat to go. Engineers made a garment that had three layers. Many tubes were connected to a water tank. Cold water circulated through the fabric. It prevented sweating. It also stopped helmets from fogging up. It was called a liquid cooling system.

This blue suit uses a liquid cooling system.

Space suits are tested in a large **vacuum** chamber, which is like being in space.

Space Shuttle Program (1972–2011)

In 1975, the Space Race came to an end. NASA sent an Apollo spacecraft into space and docked it with a Soviet ship. There, in space, a U.S. astronaut and a Soviet **cosmonaut** shook hands. The two rivals began to work together.

Not long before that, NASA started a new program. They wanted to build a ship that could be reused. Up until then, spacecraft would land in water after flights. Each ship could only be used one time. A spacecraft that could be used over and over would make space travel much less expensive. They called this new spacecraft a space shuttle.

The first space shuttle flew in 1981. Over the next 30 years, there were 135 space shuttle flights. One of the biggest jobs for these astronauts was to build a space station. The International Space Station (ISS) took more than a thousand hours to build. This led to many space suit changes to keep astronauts safe.

A glove is tested in a vacuum.

The space shuttle *Discovery* sends astronauts to build the ISS in 1984.

An astronaut tests new tools for space in a desert on Earth.

An astronaut tests the SAFER system.

TECHNOLOGY

SAFER

Another device engineers made was a small jet pack. It had nitrogen **thrusters**. These thrusters could propel an astronaut through space. It was called SAFER and could only be used for a short time. It was meant only for emergencies. If an astronaut was separated from a shuttle, he or she could use SAFER to get back. SAFER was not a typical technology. It was built with the hope that it would never have to be used.

Scientists have been able to improve space suits. Current suits are two pieces. The upper part is made of a hard material. It holds all the electrical parts, cooling system, and life support. It also has an Apollo-style helmet. The lower half of the suit is more flexible. The soft parts of the suit become firm when oxygen is pumped through it. There are 11 layers of material. They are sewn and glued together. These suits are made of different parts. They are put together to make one suit.

Though the suits are safe, they are not very flexible. Astronauts must be able to twist in the suits the way they would in regular clothes. This is the biggest problem that scientists are trying to solve. How can a space suit be more flexible while still keeping the person inside safe?

Astronaut Sandra Magnus puts on a practice suit to train before helping to build the ISS.

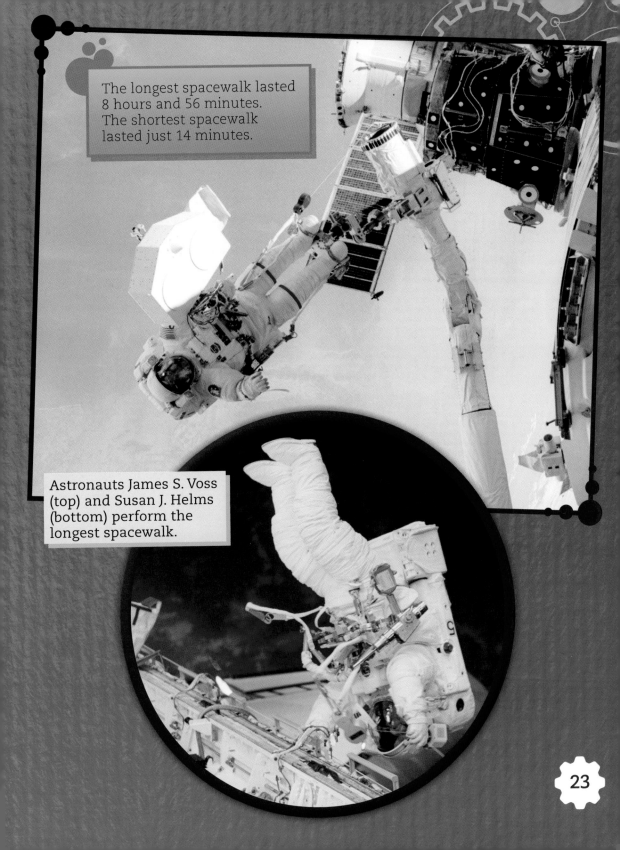

The longest spacewalk lasted 8 hours and 56 minutes. The shortest spacewalk lasted just 14 minutes.

Astronauts James S. Voss (top) and Susan J. Helms (bottom) perform the longest spacewalk.

Looking to the Future

The U.S. space shuttle program is over, but NASA still has big plans for the future. Many of these plans involve sending astronauts farther into space than ever before. One of NASA's goals is to send a crew to Mars.

These missions would require more changes to space suits. Astronauts will have to spend even more time in space. Many scientists have designed suits that they think will work best for future space travel. Some are hard shells on the outside. Others are soft and flexible. Each design has its strengths and weaknesses.

One of NASA's designs is called the Z-2. It is much lighter and more **durable** than current space suits. Another suit is called the PXS. It is designed to have parts made using a 3-D printer. This would allow astronauts to make new parts for their suits when they need them instead of having to bring extra pieces.

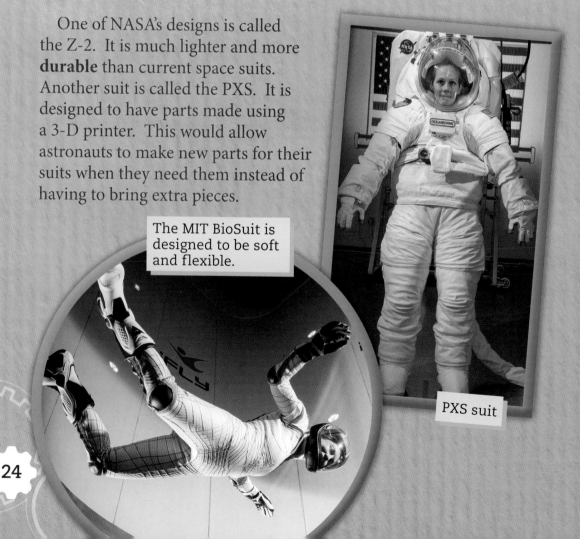

The MIT BioSuit is designed to be soft and flexible.

PXS suit

Z-2 suit

Fashion Contest

When making the Z-2 suits, NASA decided to try something new. It held a contest. Fashion students were asked to create the suit's outer layer. They had to think about the technical parts, too. The public then voted for its favorite. The winning design is gray with red patches. The patches give off light. This helps NASA monitor astronauts when they are outside of the space shuttles.

Astronauts have been able to do many things in space. They have done spacewalks. They have walked on the moon. They have learned much about our solar system. All those things would not have been possible without space suits.

Thanks to engineers, people are able to travel to space safely. They have helped make the impossible happen. Space suits have come a long way. From the first suits used for the Mercury missions to the latest suits being tested by NASA, there have been great improvements.

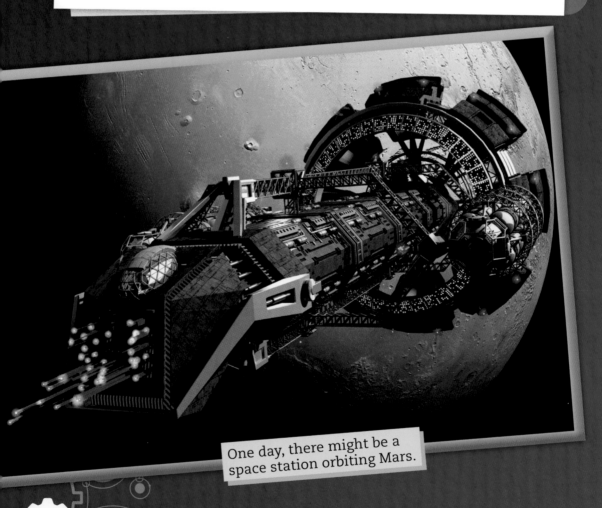

One day, there might be a space station orbiting Mars.

The look and function of space suits may have evolved over time, but the reason for them has always been the same. Space suits are designed to keep people safe. They help people travel to space and return home safely. No matter how they look, that will always be what is most important.

NASA hopes to send astronauts to Mars.

Putting on a space suit is called *donning* a suit. Removing the suit is called *doffing*.

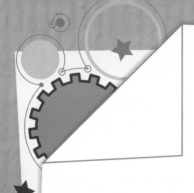

STEAM CHALLENGE

Define the Problem

NASA is continually upgrading space suits to make astronauts safe from space dust and debris. Your task is to design a protective layer for a space suit. The layer should protect an "astronaut" (represented by an object such as a marshmallow, inflated balloon, potato, or something similar) from "space dust and debris" (represented by rocks, gravel, nails, or similar items).

Constraints: Your protective layer must be made of five materials or less.

Criteria: Your protective layer should not break when $\frac{1}{2}$ liter (about 2 cups) of debris is dropped on it. Your layer can be punctured, as long as the astronaut stays unharmed.

Research and Brainstorm

How have space suits changed over time to keep astronauts safe? What materials have the best chance of keeping your astronaut safe from debris? What other factors should be considered while designing the protective layer?

Design and Build

Sketch your design, including measurements for each part of your protective layer. Build the model.

Test and Improve

Place your protective layer around your astronaut. Drop different types of space dust and debris onto your protective layer. How did your layer hold up? Did any debris get to your astronaut? Modify your design and try again.

Reflect and Share

Remember, space dust and debris travel at great speeds. Knowing that, how might you make your test more realistic? Would other types of materials provide different results? Explain what types of materials might make your protective layer better.

Glossary

abort—to stop something before it is completed because of problems or danger

altitudes—heights above the level of the sea

cosmonaut—a Soviet or Russian astronaut

durable—staying in good condition over a long period of time

life support—equipment or materials needed to keep a person alive where life is usually not possible

lunar—relating to Earth's moon

maneuver—a skilled action or movement

nylon—a strong material that is used in the making of fabrics and plastics

range of motion—full movement potential of a body part

spacewalks—activities performed by astronauts outside spacecrafts

thrusters—engines that produce forward or upward pushes by discharging jets of fluid or streams of particles

vacuum—an empty space in which there is no air or other gases

wet suits—types of clothing that are worn in cold water to keep people warm